Dedication

First and foremost I'd like to dedicate this book to my best friend and love of my life Linzi.

Linzi, I thank you for helping me get 12,000 jumbled up words out of my head and onto paper!

I'd also like to thank Zac & Kitty for being the best children a father could ask for.

And finally I thank all of you that have made this book possible.

I

Published by Peer House Publishing,

3, Newfield Road,
Newhaven,
East Sussex,
BN9 9ND

ISBN: 978-0-9926466-0-8

Photography & Design by: Kingsley @ www.kingsleybarker.com

The
Hairy Arsed
Builder's Guide
To
Stress Management

Dave Lee

INTRODUCTION

A few years ago, I was really into self-development books. They have, and probably still do have, a profound impact on me and the beliefs and values I carry with me.

After a while though, I started to realise that these books were like houses. They were all made essentially of the same old stuff: foundations, walls, floors and a roof, with drainage and electrical services running through, but perhaps just assembled in a slightly different way to each other, to a different size, perhaps with a slightly different aspect, and finished in a different material, whether it be brick, glass, timber, slate or concrete.

Fundamentally, however, they were all doing the same job, in the same way, using all the same tools and aimed at the same housing market: the safe-bet, high-volume, middle-aged, middle-England, literate, solvent world of the middle-class homeowner. And there are countless amounts of them: the 'Chicken Soups' and the '7- Habits', to the 'Awaken the Giant' genre of books. Whilst all well-meaning and written with a clear message of how we can live a better and fuller life, there is one common factor that they all share, and it is that they require a fundamental understanding of the language and style of the world from which the writer is coming.

To my mind, there is a reason for that, and it is fundamentally that the book business is managed and run, by well-read, well-educated, middle-tier, homeowners who have what seems to be a safe, universal, tried-and-tested view of the language and style that constitutes a book worthy of publication, and of course, one that will make money.

So, what about the rest of the world? The rest of the world that constitutes everywhere outside of the middle-class housing estates of suburban middle-England? Who is writing in the language and style understood by the world of the Victorian back-to-back, the post-war prefabricated Airy, the 60s high rise, and the 30s semi? To my knowledge, there isn't anyone.

That is, at least, until earlier this week, when I was asked to read and review 'The Hairy Arsed Builder's Guide to Stress Management', by Dave Lee.

One of the all time great self-development writers Dale Carnegie once wrote: "I am very fond of strawberries and cream, but I have found that for some strange reason, fish prefer worms. So when I went fishing, I didn't think about what I wanted. I thought about what they wanted. I didn't bait the hook with strawberries and cream. Rather, I dangled a worm or grasshopper in front of the fish."

And it seems to me, whether Lee is aware of it or not, that Carnegie's strategy for choosing his bait for fishing, is precisely the strategy that Lee followed when he wrote this book. Whilst it is clear that he knew precisely who his audience was from the outset, what I don't think he knows is just how many more people besides the Hairy Arsed Builder will 'get' this book, and the message that he does so brilliantly to convey in his unique, loveable and intimate style.

There are so many things I love about this book, and that make it so attractive to his audience: the builder's vernacular style of language in which it is written throughout; the metaphors – "Being ungrateful can be like looking at 40 tonnes of topsoil that needs to be wheelbarrowed uphill, it starts raining, and your mates haven't turned up to help." – the slightly chaotic way in which some of the sections are written to get the message across; the depth and intimacy of his own personal life experiences that Lee shares with the reader to reinforce the points he is making; and beyond it all, the bottom line is: it all works, and the penny drops.

The Hairy Arsed Builder's Guide to Stress Management is aptly and perfectly titled:

It does everything that it says on the tin.

Essentially the book is a DIY guide to manage the way in which we think about our everyday 'stuff' in a more effective way.

The book takes us on a journey of some of the key issues that Lee sees (representing, in my opinion, the working class of 21st Century Britain, in its collective belief systems that it carries around self-worth, and resultant behaviours deriving there from) to be a particular cause of why we live life in so much stress and pain.

He then suggests ways in which we can resolve them, by referring to his strategies as 'tools in the toolbox'. These tools, he tells the reader, are available throughout the working day, and what is more, they are simple to use, immediately effective and cost nothing.

The brilliance of this book is that it takes the reader on a real and honest, sometimes laugh-out-loud funny, and at other times, a rough and ready journey of truth about work, money, and the human condition in the passenger seat of a freezing cold white transit van on a pissing wet murky Monday morning in October.

Every bit of it I can relate to from a deeply humble, practical, gritty grass roots view of the trials of life in working class 21st Century Britain: "My mind was like an old cement mixer going round and round..."

This book is a work of sacrifice; sacrifice of himself, as he shares his own 'journey' to the outside world. And of love, as he dedicates the book to and for the benefit of those like Lee himself: those with whom he works, sees, feels and touches whilst digging footings on the building site, or stuck in traffic in the van next to his on the M25, or propping up the trade counter at the builder's merchants every day.

Dale Carnegie also said: "The ideas I stand for are not mine. I borrowed them from Socrates. I swiped them from Chesterfield. I stole them from Jesus. And I put them in a book. If you don't like their rules whose would you use?"

Similarly, there is nothing that Lee has written in 'The Hairy Arsed Builder's Guide to Stress Management' that is new.

What is new about this book, is the audience at which it is aimed, and how it is written. No Canfield, Hanson, Covey or Robbins, with all of their bachelor degrees and education, could ever have conceived such a work, or indeed ever will. This book has the potential of causing a revolution. A revolution of thinking in the streets, closes and terraces of everyday working Britain, make no doubt about it.

Jim Ogden
Property Developer

Upon reading this book I am instantly compelled to reflect and delve into the depths of my mind toolbox, extracting tools that have been rusting away in my subconscious for years, lost and neglected.

I am now cleaning these old tools and realising their power and significance in making my world a better place.

I have known Dave for quite some years now as my employer and as a friend, I witnessed his lows and the highs and he never fails to shock or amaze me. I am empowered by his transformation of character in recent years, his positive energy, dedication, passion, love for life and the universe. The big man is an inspiration to me and many others he touches.

It has been an honour and a privilege to help with the visuals of this book and I endorse it wholeheartedly. We must all honour our own magnificence, life is a gift, embrace it don't fight it.

Kingsley Barker
Professional Film-Maker and Photographer

Dave Lee

CONTENTS

PLANNING

I'm Dave, I'm a builder, and I'm also on a journey to find peace of mind. I know, the two images don't often go hand in hand!

Whilst I've been on this journey of self-discovery I happen to have found some tools along the way that I'd like to share with you.

Consider this a builder's guide on how to find peace of mind. This guide is here to offer you an opportunity to try a different way of thinking. Its intention is to help you achieve peace of mind and a happier way of life.

As anyone who has ever attempted any DIY or building work will tell you, having the right tools for the job is essential. With the start of any project there's the setting out, the making of plans, and picturing the outcome.

Plans are what guide us through the process of whatever it is we're trying to create. Say, for instance, that you were going to put a room in the roof or dig out your basement; you would need drawings and maybe planning permission. You create the drawings so you have a guide and day by day, with hard work and effort the room or extension starts to take shape.

Planning for home improvements or any building work is just like being on the journey to finding peace of mind. I found making a set of plans helpful. You wouldn't leave major home improvements to chance, so why is it we leave our own wellbeing to chance? If you want to find peace of mind, try writing a 'Vision for Yourself' – it's the surest way to get the job done.

You could take this time now to write a vision for yourself of what you would like to become, relationships you'd like to improve, old habits you'd like to let go of, parts of yourself you'd like to change, or maybe a project you'd like to start. I found writing down my visions for change really helpful at the beginning of my journey as they gave me something concrete to focus on. You don't need to show anyone else this 'Vision Statement' if you feel a bit silly, it's totally private to you. I actually put mine in a sealed envelope so no one else could see it.

I wrote down that I wanted to be loving, lovable and loved. I needed to take myself less seriously, because back then, wow was I a grumpy specimen. I wanted to be a kind and loving dad, not the snappy and remote father I often was. I wanted to be free of the black moods that had plagued me for so many years, and all the stress my behaviour and attitude were causing to myself and others.

The remarkable thing I found is that when I opened my envelope after a period of time, I had achieved all of the above 'Visions' (and more) and I had done so by changing only one small thing – my thinking.

If you take time now to write down your list of 'self improvements', you're allowing yourself to become free of what stresses you out and gets you down or keeps you from being happy. You can either do a bad job or a good one. There's no site agent or Foreman on this job to guide you, everything is to be done by you. You draw the plans and create the vision that feels right for you.

So if you're feeling angry, sad, bitter, jealous, stressed and depressed or if you're wallowing in self pity, try changing that thought. It's the thoughts you're thinking right now in this moment that make you feel like all of the above – and that's all they are, thoughts. We can change these if we choose to do so. We control them, they do not control us. If you're regularly experiencing these negative thoughts and emotions then it's likely the old tools you have in your 'Mind Tool Box' are no longer working for you. It's time to get some new tools that actually work and do the job properly, which is just a rather long-winded way of saying *CHANGE THE WAY YOU THINK!*

You wouldn't use a screwdriver to dig a hole would you? It's the same with our thinking. You won't become happier by thinking downbeat thoughts. Sound like common sense? I know, but whoever said common sense was common. I know from experience that having a head full of bleak and miserable thoughts, and at the same time having feelings of being happy just can't be done, the two just don't go together. Like oil and water, dark thoughts and being cheerful don't mix.

When you become even a tiny bit more open to changing the way you think, you'll find that you naturally become more accepting and patient of other people and situations that life throws at you, but most importantly and above all else you'll be more accepting of yourself. Come to the realisation that it's not about changing the outside world, because let's face it, as much as we'd like to change everything and everybody around us, we can't. Instead we can change the world within, changing the way we alone think.

It's like when they swapped cement from 50kg to 25kg bags. It became easier to do the job. The load become lighter, as does the load in your head when you shift your thinking.

Be aware that when you do the work required to find peace of mind, there are bound to be pitfalls and set-backs. Liken it to going down to the builders merchants with a list of materials for a job: you've got wood, wallpaper and screws written down on that list. Then you get home and discover that the wood is the wrong size, that there's not enough wallpaper and the screws are too short. It's irritating, but these things are sent to try us. Just like learning to achieve peace of mind, situations will be sent to test and challenge you.

Making yourself mindful of the likelihood of these situations cropping up is the first step in overcoming them. Like the Site Agent with a bee in his bonnet, you know the one, always picking fault and yelling. What you need to remember though is that there's no

Site Agent or Foreman in the land who has spoken to you worse than you've spoken to yourself.

I think we are all guilty of being our own worst critic. Ask yourself the question: would you speak to your best friend the way you sometimes speak to yourself? Negative self-talk is so exhausting. A simple tool to implement is just to try and talk to *yourself* in a kind manner.

When we start to be kinder and more loving to ourselves, life starts to become easier and eventually far less stressful. We become more tolerant of ourselves and kinder to others. The job of living becomes easier. Eventually the new positive mindset replaces the old pessimistic one.

Think about this: when you complete a job, you love the praise that comes from others for doing something well, but we often don't want to hear it or believe it when it comes from the most important person – ourselves. We can be so self-critical. This 'self-talk' is very draining. Like the leaky tap or badly fitted door that lets the heat out, negative self-talk is an energy drain. There's no cavity fill or insulation grant to fix this bad-boy. The secret to stopping this drain in energy lies within us and only we have the power to change a pessimistic thought into an optimistic one.

Are you ready to change the way you think?

MIND TOOL BOX

Write a vision for yourself.

Notice the way you talk to yourself. If you wouldn't talk to your mate that way, don't talk to yourself like it!

Learn to be patient with yourself.

Try random acts of kindness towards yourself or others.

Be honest with yourself.

Don't put contempt before investigation.

FOUNDATIONS

One of the greatest pleasures I get from my job is driving through the gates of a new building site. I get given a set of drawings that act as a guide to where the new building should go. I have a date for completion, a gang of men, and a shed full of tools. I'm introduced to the Site Agent and after that I'm left to decide on a daily basis what tools I should use, much like the tools I've discovered on my 'other' journey.

Some days the tools will work, the job flows great and other days they don't.

As a Ground Work Foreman most of what I do is not seen by Joe Public, it's all below ground. You drive on the roads we construct, your house sits on the foundations we laid, you flush your toilet down the drains we have installed, the house is heated by the electric or gas services we helped place and water flows in and out of your house through the pipes we put in. The foundations are the most important though, for without good foundations the house will collapse.

Like the tools we use for peace of mind, these services benefit our day-to-day lives, quietly and unobtrusively, under the surface.

Just as having a warm house, flowing hot water and a decent flushing toilet makes life easier and more pleasurable, so does experiencing peace of mind. It makes living with yourself and others a great deal easier.

However, it would be wrong to presume that there aren't days when I might struggle to stay positive There are some days I go to my tool shed and nothing works, my tools are broken or not where they're supposed to be. It makes working on site slower, less productive and very frustrating. But it's all good, some days will be tough and some days you will be singing. There will always be the rough with the smooth.

Using the new tools you'll pick up by reading this guide will take practice and determination, especially if you haven't used them for a while or if they are new to you. Learning to drive a car takes many lessons and lots of practice before you can confidently jump in and speed off, the same applies to using these mind-tools. Believe it or not, it takes practice in learning how to be kind to yourself. We are specialists in giving ourselves a hard time; we're like the school leavers on the job for first time getting used to new ideas and being in the workplace. The thing to remember is that none of us are perfect. This is not about being better than anyone else, this is about feeling better about yourself than you currently do.

I'll confess that I found using these 'mind-tools'

strange at first, and at times downright difficult or even painful. However, there's a certain amount of pain you need to go through just before you have a personal break-through. I've heard it said that pain stands for 'Pay Attention Inside Now'. That to me means if I'm feeling down or stressed-out, look inside. What am I thinking? Can I change the thought? By becoming aware that you have the ability to change your thinking, you can change how you feel.

Someone wise once told me the definition of insanity is to keep doing the same thing over and over, expecting a different result. So, if your thoughts are not giving you the peace of mind you're after, change them. With just the simple act of changing your thoughts, life becomes a little calmer, a little more peaceful and less stressful for those around you. For me it's about finding peace of mind on a daily basis. The pleasure of life is to be had now, not sometime in the future.

I've found that being grateful is the tool I use most often. Without gratitude, the job in hand will always take longer, go wrong, or fail to live up to your expectations. It's such a powerful tool. Like a good set of drawings or gang of men that know what they're doing, gratitude can take the stress out of any job.

Being ungrateful can be like looking at 40 tonnes of topsoil that needs to be wheelbarrowed uphill, it starts raining, and your mates haven't turned up to help.

I used to wake up without gratitude, which is like assembling a flat-pack kitchen without drawings. Have you tried fitting a kitchen or even a simple set of drawers together without a set of instructions? Generally it's not a pleasurable experience. This, for me, is what life was like without gratitude.

So what is gratitude? It can't be bought, measured or weighed. It costs nothing, but it is priceless. It's about being thankful for the people, places and things in our lives that we tend to take for granted. For instance: on waking up of a morning, what is your first thought? Most people I ask say it's a downbeat one.

I spent 90% of my life waking up with thoughts like "it's cold and rainy and miserable" or "I hate Mondays!" or "I hate having to work"... you get the picture. I had a really negative mindset. I suffered depression, I wallowed in self pity and I drank far too much. I was a grumpy old man at the ripe old age of 30.

It wasn't until I met my dear friend Andrew (*www. themoderndaywizard.com*) that my concept of gratitude began to change. He told me to think of gratitude like this: imagine you're in a dark room and unable to find your way out, gratitude is the torch you can use to find your way.

I now wake every morning and say "thank you" in my head at least three times. I'm thankful for work, I'm thankful for the love of my wife Linzi and I'm thankful for the comfortable bed I've slept in. I'm even grateful for the toilet roll, imagine life without that! It's the simple things we take for granted that we should be most grateful for. Life gives us so much.

How often do you tell your loved ones that you're grateful for what they bring into your life? It's not about how we achieve it or what we do to get it. It's about being thankful and seeing what we have, rather than what we don't have. Voicing gratitude is a great way to start your day. Like when your car breaks down, you miss it. How many people get in their car and give a cheeky thanks for it being there? Anyone that has broken down in the middle of nowhere knows that feeling when the breakdown man gets you going again, it's called gratitude!

Gratitude is about being thankful. In these uncertain times how many in the morning give thanks for their job? It could be as simple as smiling at someone on the train. You smile at them, they smile back. It's the little things!

Gratitude helps the job flow more easily too, the phone will ring and friends will turn up to help move that 40 tonnes of top soil and the sun will come out. Gratitude is a ray of sunshine on a cloudy day, so enjoy using it, voicing it. Let the Universe, your friends and family and loved ones know how grateful you are for all the great things in your life, big or small. Even if you have to 'fake it to make it' as I did in the beginning, until I started to feel genuine gratitude.

Coming from a place lacking in gratitude can make life seem hard work. Do you wake up in comfort? Is there running water and heat from a flick of a switch?

How many of our creature comforts do we take for granted? Yup, loads. The mind will say: "I work hard for those comforts" and I've no doubt you do, but I read in the national geographic that in other countries people work even harder for less than a dollar a day. More than a billion people are on a dollar a day.

So have gratitude for our relatively comfortable lives compared to those folks.

MIND TOOL BOX

Start your day with gratitude, change the attitude.

Write down or bring to mind things that you're grateful for.

Think about what you have, not what you haven't.

Let those people in your life know how grateful you are for what they do. They won't know unless you tell them.

Say "thank you, thank you, thank you" when starting your day.

DRAINAGE

I used to find staring into space easy and even taking the dogs for a walk became a challenge. Work was done on auto-pilot. Being a dad and husband or friend was so difficult. I just wanted to isolate myself. When I'm in a depressed mind-set life becomes a chore and worse. My energy becomes flat; I think dark thoughts.

The feeling of depression is different for everyone and there are many different levels of feeling down. I've been all the way from merely wanting to pull the duvet over my head and stay in bed all day, curtains drawn against any light and not wanting to go to work, to almost suicidal.

I've been laid off work two weeks before Christmas. I was responsible for two small children, my wife and a mortgage; and I had no job. That can bring on a black mood to say the least. It's times like these that those thoughts around money and self worth can be really harsh and accusatory.

It's funny really. When we're happy, joyful and at peace with ourselves and the world, we don't try to fix it or label it. We enjoy the feeling that life is good. However, when we have a 'black dog day' (as Churchill famously described his depressive episodes) or in my case a couple of weeks, we try and find excuses why we're like it: "It's their fault, her fault, the car's fault, I am at fault! What's the point? " Blah, blah, blah...

I spent so much time looking for the whys and wherefores that I didn't realise I had the tools to shift the depressive feelings myself. I used to drink to excess and use drugs to try to anaesthetise myself against the pain of these black moods. They didn't work, they nearly killed me. They also nearly destroyed my family. This is why I had to go out and discover the tools for peace of mind that didn't come out of a bottle, or worse.

So, like the drainage system under your house that's set up to take away your sewage, we can let these depressive thoughts and patterns of behaviour drain away from us. We have the ability to 'catch' our depressive thoughts and deal with them. We have the choice, we can either feed them or let them go. Like two dogs fighting, whichever one you feed most will win. It's the same as the voice in your head, whichever one you listen to the most will win.

Imagine if you will that a drainage pipe breaks under your house. Sewage starts to seep in through the crack and it contaminates your home ever so slowly. The first thing you'll notice is the smell. If left overlooked, you will have a serious health risk that will need specialist help to clear up.

The thoughts that lead to depression are like that little crack. They start off being small, but gradually, slowly, they get worse. Before you know it you're overwhelmed with feeling shit (pardon the pun).

It's OK to feel down, it's all part of life and you have to take the rough with the smooth. But it's in allowing the 'feeling down' mood to pass through you that liberation lies. Like the sewage flowing through the foundations of your home without contamination, being able to let the thoughts pass by without attaching any meaning to them is the key.

Thoughts are like clouds in the sky: there's an endless stream of them always passing by, but it's whether we pull the thoughts in and give them meaning and feed them that matters.

Once these depressive thoughts come in they wipe you out. Liken them to standing in the rain on a freezing winter's morning, knee deep in mud, eight hours of hand digging to go. Not only that, your clothes are soaked, there's no drying room and you've got to sit in the back of a van with no heating. Oh and there's a two hour drive home on the M25 to look forward to after you're done digging. You constantly ask yourself "what's the point?" knowing that you get to do it all again the next day…

Somewhere inside yourself you find that energy to get out of bed and do it all again. I'm sure there are many times in your life that there's been despair. Mine is on me today as I write this, thinking "what's the point?" But with shade comes light. There are days when it's been raining, but The Boss Man says "come on, bugger this, lets go home." He pays you the shift as well – result.

The point I'm making is this: to act on a decision to push on through, even though it was pouring with rain, meant that the day had a positive outcome. I'm lifting my head and pushing on through today and I know that it's only a thought that I'm thinking. It's not real, it won't last and it's not me. *You are not your thoughts*, you have the ability to change them.

When I used to start the day with a negative thought I found it hard to contemplate my life, money and relationships. If I was lucky I might have someone in the van to share the journey to work and to take my mind off things. If not, I was stuck with my own head moaning and groaning on. Then I discovered I could change my bleak thoughts on those early mornings into positive ones. If I listen to crappy, negative thoughts I will create indecision and worry, closely followed by fear. Change the thought into a positive, grateful one and you'll see (and feel) the immediate benefits.

So, rather than leaving my thoughts and peace of mind to chance, I will set an intention for my day. Setting an intention is much like setting the SatNav in your car. You program that with an intended destination, so take your time in the morning to set a 'course of thought' for yourself. You wouldn't head off to some far flung destination with no direction and hope to get there by chance. It seems crazy, but this is how many of us start our day! Focusing on achieving peace of mind is how I start my day now. If I take a wrong turn, I come back to my point of focus.

I usually know when I'm off course because I start to have that ball of anxiety building up in my stomach. When I feel that now, I check my thought. I then reset my intent to enjoy my day. The anxiety lifts because I've changed my thoughts. That leaves me to enjoy the drive listening to music or some podcast and not my head blethering on!

If you're anything like me, you like to share your thoughts, good or bad. I've learned to share my positive thoughts, not project my negative thoughts onto family and friends or even strangers. Our nearest and dearest and members of the public don't need to know everything that goes on in our heads. It's not nice being covered in someone else's sewage. And I should know, I've been down enough blocked manholes in my time. I have been covered in someone else's sewage on a cold Monday morning. Unblocking someone's drain is a great way of learning to laugh at myself. Laughing is a great stress buster. If I had not laughed, I think I would have cried.

I've used the analogy of working in the rain. But I also know of many situations that create depression, despair, and thoughts of suicide. There are groups, doctors and helplines that you can access freely if you find yourself becoming bogged down in feelings of depression. It's nothing to be afraid or ashamed of and you're a stronger person for asking for help if it all becomes too much.

Oh and avoid hand digging in the rain...Get a machine in wherever possible!

MIND TOOL BOX

Set the SatNav within your mind daily with intent.

Check your thinking, when you wake in the morning what is your first thought – positive or negative? If your thoughts are dark and down you have the choice to turn them around.

Like the SatNav, you can always reset yourself, no matter how far down the road you've gone.

Don't let pride get in the way of asking for help.

HARD GRAFT

The feeling of fear is incredibly powerful. Even thoughts about fear can stop a grown man or woman from achieving great things in their life. Facing fear and overcoming it has been (and still can be) one of the hardest jobs I've ever tackled.

I grew up with fear being my most commonly felt emotion. I'm not talking about the 'being chased down the road by a man with a knife' kinda fear (although I've experienced that too, I'll save that story for another time), I'm talking about the fear that comes from within, created by the mind.

If you were to ask anyone what frightens them, some might say nothing. Some blokes I know say hard graft… However, if they were to be really honest with you then the answer might be lots of things. Let's name a few of those fears so as to get a good idea of what we're dealing with.

There's the fear of poverty, who is not afraid of having no money? Why do we do the jobs we do, work all the hours we can and travel long distances to find it? Because we are afraid of not having enough of it! If I had a pound for every mile travelled for work I could retire now. What makes me do that? Well it's the fear of not having it.

Fear of poverty is incredibly controlling.

There's the fear of illness or some sort of paralysing accident. There's also the fear of death, most people are afraid of dying. As we know, the only two certainties in life are death and taxes, but still it creates fear in a lot of people nonetheless. There's also the fear of growing older; mix in fear of poverty and death and you've got yourself a great fear cocktail.

There's fear around relationships. The fear of losing a relationship can create a multitude of feelings and emotions ranging from loneliness to jealousy. That fear can be a huge cause in relationship break-ups. If jealousy creeps into bed with you and your partner it's hard to find any peace of mind with jealousy creating destructive thoughts. The main fear I lived with was that I just wasn't good enough. These are unconscious, very subtle fears, but they control our very way of being and stop us achieving that precious peace of mind, even though fear is just an illusion. It's not real, it's just a thought.

The great thing is, I discovered a tool that overcomes fear. The next tool I'd like to share with you is Faith.

Faith sounds like a religious word, but it has nothing to do with any religion or going to church. It's about having belief in a positive outcome, belief in yourself and with any project you wish to start. Don't give up because your head tells you to.

Without Faith, fear creeps in like damp slowly seeping into the walls of your house. If it is left untreated, the damp can be a costly problem to get rid of. Fear, if left untreated, can cause a lifetime of negative thinking that we're often not even aware of.

Like the damp, we only become aware of it when it starts affecting our health.

I heard a great analogy the other day, that it's like driving down a country road at night, when all you can see is three white lines in front of you. You can't see bugger all but if you follow those white lines and the directions, you'll eventually get to your destination. That, my friend, is faith. Not being able to see the big picture, but trusting that all will be OK, rather than feeding the fear of not knowing.

There's a man that lives alone in a dark room. For years he has been scared of the snake in the corner; it keeps him awake at night. He's afraid to go anywhere near it. He is always thinking about that snake in the dark! One day however the lights go on for the briefest of moments. In that second he finally sees the snake for what it really is: the 'snake' is just an old piece of rope. The lights go out again, leaving the man once again alone in the dark. The man is never afraid again because he faced his fear. He saw the snake for what it was – just an imagined thought.

This is what happens when you start to question your thoughts. You get to see them for what they really are: illusions based on shadows of past events and future happenings. The real tool is to question the thought that is making you feel afraid, upset, fearful, confused, stressed or unhappy. As you start to question your thoughts the 'snake' can no longer appear real.

Imagine if I were to give you a price for some building work you required. We agree the price and I start the work. Within a week of me starting the work I send you an invoice by post. The invoice is twice as much as we agreed. You have a reaction as soon as you see the bottom line. It might be anger or fear, but either way your mind will cut in with a big story. Then, you're unable to get hold of me for two days. Your mind will be going into a big yarn of how you've been ripped off, that you're not going to pay it. You're imagining having all sorts of conversations with me. When there is no communication your mind will always make up the worst. You're so distracted that you've lost sleep, you're preoccupied at work, and you're being generally irritable to say the least.

Eventually you get hold of me. You've had two days to think of what you're going to say. You've got this whole speech worked out in your mind. I pick up the phone and say: "sorry, the phone had broken and the invoice was meant for another job, I sent it to you by mistake." Up until now the thoughts you were having stopped you enjoying anything you were doing. This is how we spend most of our lives – caught in a story.

Being able to see fear for what it is allows you to have peace of mind. The mind just likes to think it knows everything. That's why I've continued with the book, even though at times I've just wanted to rip it up. The voice of self-doubt nagging: "you're just a builder, who wants to hear your story?!" ringing in my ears, but I know the thoughts are not mine. I can't predict my next thought, can you? I'm allowing the insecurity and thoughts of low self-worth to be there, but I'm not feeding them or even attaching any importance to them.

It's being able to catch the thoughts before they run off causing havoc. They are not real! Learn to question them, ask yourself if it is real, are the thoughts you're telling yourself and others true?

MIND TOOL BOX

Faith is auto suggestion to the subconscious mind.

Face your fears and do it anyway.

Just because you think it, doesn't make it true.

Learn to question your thoughts.

DRIVING

When I had the idea for this guide I roughly drafted out the headings I wanted to write about. I pencilled in 'Driving' because if this is a DIY guide for dealing with stressful situations, then one of the most stressful has got to be driving! So I looked in my mind-tool box and found the best tool for the job. It's called Acceptance. For me it was acknowledging and accepting that everybody drives differently. Some slow, some fast, some hesitant – all the kinds of driving that frustrate me if I let them. I discovered other drivers weren't making me feel the road rage, I was.

I'm responsible for how I feel. After spending a lifetime pointing the finger of blame at others, this was a revelation. I spent so much time blaming others for making me feel this way, or that way, or any way. This revelation and breakthrough thankfully came to me before I killed someone with my bad driving.

It was once shown to me that if I'm pointing the finger of blame at someone else, then I've got three of my fingers pointing right back at me. This helped me to see that I should take a good look at myself before blaming others.

I work long, hard hours at my job as many of you do. My days are up early, home late. I get tired, I get grumpy. In the past I had no gratitude (or any of the other tools I've previously mentioned) in my mind-toolbox – my box was empty. Driving was a stressful experience that on some days would see me chasing a complete stranger down a motorway at 100mph for some perceived misdemeanour, an inch off their bumper. This was not a clever thing to do. I had no concept that other drivers could make mistakes. Oh, but it was OK for me to drive like a nutter, oh yeah. So, with the wife in the car screaming at me to slow down and behave, I carried on regardless; I didn't care that the kids were in danger or that the other road users were too.

So how can we use this wonderful tool of acceptance? For me, it's about being tolerant of where I am. For instance, if you're stuck in traffic, accept that's where you're meant to be. It's only the mind saying you should be at home, the job or somewhere else. If you were meant to be there you'd be there already! Accept that no one is perfect, we all make mistakes, we all have things on our mind that take our attention off the road. They say most driving is done by the subconscious mind anyway.

This is another little tool that helps; if you are cut up by another driver, think of it as negativity getting away from you. Let them (and their negativity) go, you don't have to chase them.

I'll give you this example: we finish work and within a mile of leaving the site the person I'm with starts complaining about the other road users' bad driving. The next thing you know, cars start cutting us up and near misses are happening all over the show. It's turning out to be quite a stressful journey really. What's happening is that my driver is attracting these dreadful drivers due to him focusing all of his energy on them. If you keep thinking about bad drivers, don't be surprised if they come out of the woodwork, because that's what you're attracting in!

The way to stop this in its tracks is to bring your attention back on how *you're* driving, sing along to the radio, etc. Break the train of thought that's focusing on the other driver's skills (or lack thereof), It's not your problem. If you're the passenger in one of the vehicles I've mentioned here then it's a scary and stressful experience. Driving doesn't have to be stressful and road rage kills. Aggressive driving scares the kids and other road users. It certainly doesn't get you there any quicker and it can destroy lives in an instant, and for what? You're allowing your thinking and emotions to be controlled by another's actions. That's madness.

Take responsibility for the way you act and feel. You and you alone control your emotions. What gives us the right to become judge and jury over a perceived wrongdoing at a road junction in the middle of nowhere?

The other great tool I use when driving is 'letting go'. I'll use this analogy: On a building site many years ago there were two bricklayers. These bricklayers were only ever paid to lift and lay bricks. One day, a young chippy asked the bricklayers for a hand. The younger of the two said: "yes of course" and that he would be happy to help. The older man mumbled to himself and turned his back to carry on laying his bricks. The younger man went off to help carry some timber that supported the roof, which took ten minutes of his time. The chippy thanked him and they both got on with their jobs. After the bricklayers had finished their shift they were getting changed in the drying room. The older bricklayer said to the young bricklayer that it wasn't right that he helped carry the timber for the chippy. The young man turns to the older and says to him: "I put that timber down six hours ago, why are you still carrying it?"

Wow, to let something go is so liberating! Instantly there is calm and a sense of ease back in the car. Before the alleged incident or wrongdoing by a fellow road user there was a calm, loving family man or woman. They were on their way for a nice day out with the family. But if you don't 'let go', well now there's a lunatic driving the car, full of road rage.

I'm so glad I discovered the tools that allow me to have a pleasant drive, so thankfully I don't have scenes like that any more (and the wife screams at me far less often!).

Remember, as with all the tools I suggest, they are only *suggestions.* But by using them regularly, a sense of inner peace will come. Traffic will flow, stress levels will go down and the family will become more relaxed. You will also say sorry a lot less. I spent half my life saying "sorry". The amount of flowers I've bought and cards I've written bearing that worn out word. Now I buy flowers for the pleasure of giving them and not to make it up to a furious wife.

Changing the way you think creates action. You end up doing things differently. You can't keep hitting a nail with a 14lb sledge hammer, eventually something has to give. It's going to get very painful holding the nail and your thumb will thank you for it.

The peace of mind you get by using these tools is incredible. They become second nature after a while, and you'll know when you're not using them because you'll begin to feel angry, frustrated, stressed, and fearful again.

You'll also start having to say sorry again. Are you not bored with being that way? You get fed up feeling sorry for yourself and of upsetting other people.

It's like when you have a stone in your shoe. You move your foot, arch and shuffle it around trying to get comfortable. Eventually you have to take your shoe off and chuck out the stone.

It's time to pick the right tool for the job. Change the way you have been doing it and feel comfortable within yourself. The great thing about these tools is that they create a ripple effect on everyone we come into contact with.

People start to notice the change in you and when

this happens you get to give your tools away. This then creates a way of you keeping them, the more you share them, the more they work for you. One of the reasons I wanted to share them with you is so that I can remind myself I have them!

MIND TOOL BOX

Be aware of your point of focus.

Give yourself praise when doing things differently.

You control your emotions, they are your responsibility, no one else's.

Look at your hand as you point, there is always three fingers pointing back!

Your outside world ALWAYS reflects how you feel inside.

Bills, Bills And More Bills

When there are bills to pay and materials to buy, the feeling of being swamped and 'in over our heads' can be overwhelming. There's that sense that more money seems to be going out than coming in. The way we think about money can lead to countless stressful situations. Arguments, fear, depression, stress and worry come out in a multitude of ways – not sleeping, not eating, etc. Money worries are the cause of many marriage break ups. We upset those closest to us, causing the kids to panic. Generally if you have money worries you are not a nice person to be around.

I've discovered that the more I worry about money the more money worries I seem to have. Nevertheless, one thing's for sure, I never got any richer worrying about it.

I used go to the cash machine every week to check my bank balance, with that nervous thought and sense of dread in the pit of my stomach. "Oh no! I'm broke again!" I used to huff under my breath as I looked at the overdraft figures flashing on the screen. I'd only just got paid; I knew I would have to feed the family on bread and water all week. But as we know, kids need feeding and Mum needs her bits – bread and water would not do. The building game was booming some years ago and I was earning good money. I had all the perks: a big four wheel drive, bonuses, phone and holiday pay. But I didn't have peace of mind. The more I earned, the more I spent. No matter how much I earned, it was never enough. However, because I was coming from a place of lack and a place of fear I could never seem to earn enough and I was always overdrawn. I didn't realise that it was my thinking that was the problem, not the money.

I hadn't being given the right tools to deal with it. There was always an underlying fear around money in my house as I grew up, so when I started earning good money as a Foreman, I hoped against hope that the good times would last. I would spend money, earn money, spend it again, and then constantly worry about not having enough. My mind was like an old cement mixer going round and round. I was basing my happiness on my wages and how much money I had. My moods fluctuated like my bank account.

I was a slow learner and being stubborn didn't always get me what I wanted. I finally realised that I would have to change the tool I was using around money. The tool I was using wasn't working...because I didn't have one.

So changing the way I thought about money has taken away the fear I had surrounding it and with that came a balanced account and a proper night's sleep. Discovering the tool to use around money was quite literally priceless. My cash flow no longer controls me or fills me with dread. I now sleep in my own bed at night and I no longer have that horrible gut feeling whenever the bank statement hits the floor. I've stopped going to the cash point and driving myself mad, much like a dog chasing its tail.

I discovered a tool that I now try to use every time I do a transaction or have a fearful thought about money. The tool is called Affirmation. Affirmation means to keep repeating a phrase to oneself over and over to help it sink in.

It got pointed out to me I was already doing that when I had fear surrounding money – by repeating to myself that I had no money I was affirming that I didn't! The great thing is that it works the other way too. I can repeat to myself an affirmation that's positive. You could try this one for instance:

'Money flows easily and frequently to me'

It seems a mouthful to start with and you might feel like a bit of a numpty doing it, but humour me. My point is this: using this mind tool has taken the fear out of money. Of course I'm not running round with credit cards, booking holidays and buying new cars. But I am walking around with peace of mind in my wallet, and that can't be bought for any amount of cash. Peace of mind costs nothing and is given freely, which also means the wife is happier and the kids are learning to have a healthier approach to money than I had when I was growing up.

The use of affirmations creates a sense of peace around thoughts of money. My experience since using positive affirmations is that new jobs pop up unexpectedly, just when a current run of work is due to end. So instead of dropping down into a place of fear about running out of work (and consequently, cash), I instead trust that work will always come.

Don't lie in bed feeling sorry for yourself and feeding the fear. If your mind becomes blocked, clear the blockage with some different thoughts of possibility thinking. Try coming from a place of faith and trust that everything will work out and that your needs will always be met.

I don't know how this stuff works but it does! I have just had a bank statement this morning and I am in the black. I'm on the same money and still have the same outgoings. The only thing that has changed is my thinking around money. So my relationship with the wife is more relaxed, the kids are happy and I sleep at night. I'm so grateful for the money I earn after a year on the dole because I know what it's like to have none.

Like any tool, you can use the old one that's familiar (albeit a bit dodgy) or you can choose a new one that does the job better. I'll leave this chapter here because if your head's like mine it will soon find something else to worry about and get stressed over.

MIND TOOL BOX

Suggested Affirmations:

'Money flows easily and frequently to me.'

'Everything I need shall be provided today.'

'Work is easily found and my books are overflowing',

'I let my money worries slip away as I have a happy day.'

'Peace of mind cannot be bought, it costs nothing.'

WORK IN PROGRESS

Having been in the building game for over twenty years I've chased work, worried about it, lost sleep over it and travelled miles to get to it. I've felt underpaid, under appreciated and wanted to walk off jobs. I've had tantrums, walked off-site, enjoyed it, been out of work and felt deep satisfaction for a job well done. Every kind of emotion and feeling possible has risen out of me over my paid employment. I've been a labourer, a Foreman, a lackey and a tea boy. I've swept the floor and run four million pound jobs. There is so much to learn and take in within the construction industry, just when you think you've got it sussed, you're given a job you've never done before.

Being at peace with yourself can seem like that at times. There will always be challenges that will try and shatter your peace of mind. Life is like a construction site. There is always something new to learn and as one job is completed, another one comes in. Being able to keep your head when you feel the world is out to get you is a job in itself.

Have you ever seen the documentary where the polar bear is trying to get at the birds eggs? The birds defend their eggs by continually dive-bombing the bear and eventually the bear gives up. There's an image of the bear lying there with his paws over his head. I imagine he's saying "That's enough! Stop! Leave me alone!"

When days are like that and it feels like the world is out to get you, I find using a mantra helpful. This can be any well loved phrase you remember and use to get you through a difficult situation. Using a mantra has helped me achieve peace of mind when there has been nothing but chaos around me. The mantra I like is:

"No matter where I am, no matter what happens, and no matter who I'm with, the most important thing is I stay happy, calm and relaxed"

I repeat that to myself over and over. The birds with their sharp beaks can't get in then. And neither do I have to lie down on the floor with my hands over my head.

Stress is caused by our reaction to a situation. My personal experience of stress is that it was never caused by just one thing. I've always found it to be caused by a multitude of incidents and occurrences. They slowly build up like the snagging list as the job nears completion. The client starts asking: "can you do this?" and "have you finished that?" The little jobs start to pile up and you start to overstretch yourself. Trying to please everyone becomes an impossible task.

You start getting frustrated and annoyed with yourself. The little jobs suddenly become difficult and they may take longer. Frustration upon frustration compounds to create anger and it's how we react to the anger that is so important for our peace of mind.

The way I've dealt with it in the past was by erupting in a fit of rage at what appeared to be the slightest thing. Expressing your rage is a fantastic way of dealing with it in the short term, but unfortunately it's who's on the receiving end of it that matters and that causes the damage. To bottle up anger and to not express it can be so damaging. The thoughts created by anger do harm to your peace of mind and even your body more than you realise. It's been proven that our thoughts create toxins which can actually poison us. I live in a coastal town with cliff tops and I've learnt to take my anger and rage up the cliffs and express it there safely with no one at the end of it.

Say you've fallen out with someone and had a huge argument. You're filled with angry thoughts that might be keeping you awake at night, fuming and raging and far from happy. Consider this: the person you're cross with isn't affected at all by your internal thoughts. The person is at Thorpe Park having the time of their life for all you know. You don't have to show them your anger. Your anger isn't hurting them…it's hurting *you*. Whenever you look back over an angry incident, it was never about the person, it's usually about a series of events that, when layered upon each other, create a build up of anger leading to an explosion. Stress comes from avoiding or not dealing with life's little problems and allowing them to spiral out of control.

Start by being honest with yourself when you need help. I've spoken to a contract manager who has had managers off sick with stress. He told me the workload does not disappear when the person is off sick, it gets spread around others, causing them more stress. So don't leave it until it's too late, flag it up when you feel that you're starting to lose control.

Learning the tools to cope with everyday situations is the way to a calm, happy, relatively stress-free life. Don't allow the little things to build up like a snagging list. The to-do list will only get bigger. Deal with the problems as they come in and don't put off what you can do today until tomorrow. This is your peace of mind and wellbeing we're talking about.

Learning to be kind to yourself and speak your truth in the moment stops the little things building up at work, indoors or wherever you are. Flying off the handle or storming off somewhere to calm down is a sign that lots of little things are becoming one big thing.

When anger and frustration are upon us, we say and do things that we regret afterwards. Resentments, frustration, anger, jealousy and fear all contribute to reaching boiling point. Someone said the other day that stress is like the frog put in cold water and slowly boiled – eventually it dies. But if you put a frog in boiling water it jumps straight out. It's never one thing that causes stress, it's a combination of factors that slowly bring you to the boiling point. Being humble enough to ask for help is a great tool. Before I started this journey I thought I knew everything. As a Foreman running million pound jobs there wasn't much I didn't know. That was another thing I learnt the hard way – I knew nothing. I'm a little wiser now, but I'm still humble enough to ask when I don't know something or I'm struggling with some emotional problem. This is a work in progress, it's not a one-tool fix-all.

Be an adult. Talk about what's going on with someone you trust. Try to avoid getting into gossiping about others, as being judgemental is a sure-fire way to build up little frustrations and resentments.

I'm learning what it is to be free of my own judgements on myself and others. As a teenager growing up, I came into contact with more than a few judges I can tell you. I would stand in front of them in the dock for a few minutes as they told me what they thought would be a fitting punishment. But the judge I have had to work on the most is the one inside of me. I have been so judgemental of myself. I spent over half my life judging myself, giving self-imposed chastisement for things that, in the light of awareness, meant nothing. I believe we judge ourselves so harshly.

We expect so much of ourselves and are so hyper-critical. Let the person, thing or places be the way they are. You can't change them, so let it go!

The thing to remember is that no matter who I'm with, what I'm doing or where I am, the most important thing for me is that I stay relaxed, calm and happy.

I have, and I've finally lost the nick-name 'Dave Rage'!

What stresses you out today might not tomorrow, and vice versa. Learn to be like water – ebb and flow with what life can sometimes throw at you. Allow your mind to be like the lake without a ripple on it. You're in charge of that lake. You can chuck big rocks in and ride the waves, or stand on the shore and watch the boats go by.

The great thing I've learnt is that I don't have to know what's around the corner.

MIND TOOL BOX

Learn to release anger in a controlled way.

Have your own snagging list, tick things off before they get too much.

Talk about what's going on inside you with others.

Find a mantra that works for you.

It's OK to say no rather than yes.

Get to know your limits.

TEA BREAK

Well I don't know about you but after all this thinking I could do with a sit down and a cup of tea. Having a well earned tea break is in itself a fantastic tool. It's being able to take a step back when things aren't going the way we planned. A great way to step back is to ask yourself: "Do I want to be right or do I want to be happy?" This is a great tool for being able to 'let go' when things get frustrating.

The very first time I used this tool it worked straight away. To set the scene, It was a summer's day and the wife and I had been invited to a BBQ at a friend's house. I arrived at the BBQ early without the wife to have a cup of tea and catch up with the husband of our friend. When I got there, my pal asked if I would like to go for a motorbike ride. Well of course I shot off on the bike. It wasn't planned, but I hadn't told the wife what I was up to. You know the scenario, we came back far later than we intended to. By the time I got back, Linzi was there and a wee bit upset I had done this. She believed I had planned to disappear without telling her or saying where I was going, so as you can imagine our ensuing argument created a bad atmosphere. So, like 'Who Wants To Be A Millionaire', I phoned a friend. This friend suggested I say sorry. The concept of being sorry for something

I *hadn't* done was new to me. But he asked me: "do you want to be right or do you want to be happy?" I wanted to be happy of course! So I apologised and the result was amazing. Within minutes of me saying sorry, the BBQ was once again enjoyable for all. Linzi and I were at peace again.

Arguments cause so much stress for those involved. Being around arguments growing up wasn't something I enjoyed and it did me a huge amount of damage as a child.

When I started to become aware of my arguments and the hurt I was causing my own kids, it was time to make a change. Being right never made me happy. There was a sense of smugness or 'I showed you', but not happiness. By choosing to be happy, I actually *became* happy – strange that. Sometimes through gritted teeth, nails digging into the palms of my hands and mumbling under my breath. But as time went by and the more I used it, the easier it became.

As a Foreman, a lot of my job is about being right. The problem with that is I used to take my work home with me. You can imagine that didn't go down too well with Linzi. She wanted to be right as well. We've both learnt to ask this question and with that there has been a big shift in our relationship. I also learnt to leave work outside the door.

I once heard this story about a businessman. He had worked long and hard to manage a hugely important business deal. By the end of the day the contract went through and he made a million pounds cash for his company. You can imagine how he felt – happy days! He got home that night to the wife and blurted out his magnificent news. The wife said: "that's great darling, but did you bring the milk home like I asked you to?"

Learning the balance between family life and work is essential. I used take my work home with me every night, moaning and groaning on about it. Making sure I made everyone else miserable as well. I always had enough 'stories' to tell myself to keep me feeling miserable and enough excuses to keep me from being happy. When you come to realise it's your *thoughts* that create your reality, you start to become very conscious of how powerfully your thinking affects everything that surrounds you.

I've heard it said that the hardest battle to win is the one with yourself. After years of fighting with myself and wanting to be right, it's bliss to turn around and say to myself: "you know what Dave? It's OK to be happy." A happiness that's not based on anything other than a thought I have. It sounds so simple, but it's true.

I used to think happiness could be found after some future event had happened in my life. The one I hear most (and I think we've all said it at some point in our lives) goes like this:

Person A says to Person B on a Monday morning: "How you doing?"

Person B replies: "Hmmf…I'll be OK when it's Friday."

Why wait until Friday? What's wrong with now?!

I used to base my happiness on future events, so no wonder happiness alluded me. The future isn't *real*, the only thing that is real is now. Having thoughts based on events that may or may not happen in the future, such as: When I get that car I've always wanted, when I land that new job, or when I go on holiday, *then* I'll be happy. Drop all of that like a heavy weight you've been carrying. Choose happiness NOW, in this very moment. You don't have wait for anything to happen. It's only a thought, so choose a happy, positive, *present* one.

Look at it like this: when you're mixing concrete you add the right mix of aggregates to get the right strength of concrete. If you add too much water or not enough cement, it's weak. You've got to get the mix right. Your thinking is the same – you've got to get the mix right! You wouldn't start laying bricks on concrete that is so wet or weak that the bricks sink, so don't do the same with your thoughts.

Be watchful of what you feed your mind. Blame is not a word you can use once you discover the power you have over your own happiness. It takes courage to be happy.

MIND TOOL BOX

Find the courage to let it go, whatever *it* is!

Let go of always needing to be right.

Does always being 'right' make you happy?

Do the opposite of what your head tells you.

Happiness is a choice.

Learn to balance work and home life

Be happy now, not on Friday!

DECORATING

After all the hard work that's gone into the job, there's a sense of satisfaction that comes when the decorators finally come in. You can see an end to the noise, mess and chaos. You have a beautiful new space to live in at last!

The old furniture looks out of place though...if you're after a new look you're going to have to get rid of the old stuff and go shopping for some new bits.

It's the same with your thinking. You can shuffle those old thoughts around, but to have a new outlook you're going to need to change your thinking.

Talk about shopping, as I write it's now three weeks until Christmas. This time of year sees people who are lucky enough never to brave the shops, forced out of their comfort zones and into shopping centres fit to burst with harassed customers.

Stress levels rise a notch or two in these places. Big crowds, parking, traffic, queues in shops, queues to get in, queues to get out, older people, kids in tow, spending money – I'm feeling stressed even writing about it! It's enough to send any man over the edge, or woman, for that matter.

So what tools do we have that can ease the stress or pressure of the dreaded shopping experience? Patience and Tolerance. Don't forget, I was a man of so little Patience that I would spend an hour mooching around in a shop, choose what I wanted, walk to the checkout, look at the size of the queue and just put my goods down and walk right back out rather than queue up.

Today I took my children to my local shopping centre. We shopped all day looking for a Christmas dress (not for me I might add, I don't have the legs for dresses), a mission that took me into all sorts of shops to find what we were after. I used Patience and Tolerance lots and often. The trip started with me getting stuck at the barrier of a multi-storey car park because the machine had broken. I waited patiently for a man to fix it, with cars queued behind me honking their horns.

Not so long ago that would have ruined my day. Previously, I would've been out of my car like a shot, right in the faces of the people honking me, regardless of there being any kids in the vehicle or anyone else present. In fact, I didn't care who saw me go mad. I would have been complaining and arsey, upsetting the kids, ruining their trip.

However, I now use these tools as coping mechanisms for stressful situations. I no longer react like that and the benefit to those around me is amazing. There's a gentle breeze rather than a hurricane of temper. So on this day of being stuck at the barriers, not being able to move, of being angrily honked at by other drivers... I let it go, and that was that.

I recently bought my son a pair of branded trainers, they cost enough and I was a bit cheesed off that within a short period of time the sole was hanging off. So, rather than going up into the town, demanding a new pair of shoes and getting angry (as of course was my normal behaviour in years gone by) I decided to try a different approach.

I said to my lad: "We're going to ask for the shopkeepers help, we're not going to go in demanding." Instead of going in, shoulders back and slamming the shoes on the counter, I asked him to go in there with the positive intention of receiving a brand new pair of shoes. So, we asked for help and the lady explained why they were falling apart. It was due to the way my boy had been getting them on and off, it was human error rather than product quality. The lady was great and gave us a new pair of shoes, everyone was happy.

Stepping back and focusing on the positive outcome has enriched my life so much. People want to help when they're approached. It's such a simple tool to ask rather than demand. To approach gently rather than attack.

As your own mind tool box grows and you become more comfortable using the tools within, you may slowly take the 'old behaviour tools' you've been using down to the proverbial tip. You might be reluctant to let go of them because one day you might need them – but I don't think you will.

With the tools that change your thinking, letting go of the old tools will become easier. You begin to realise you don't have to struggle with them anymore. It will dawn on you that these tools can be used all the time, in any situation, not just the scenarios used in this book.

For me, it's about using all of the new tools that I've written about. No matter what job you do, be it a full time Mummy, Police Officer, Train Driver or even a White Van Man, there will be stressful situations that arise from working around others, conditions or materials, and many outside factors that are sent to try your new tool box (and Patience!)

Please remember that everything in this guide is only ever a suggestion, I don't like being told what to do, as I'm sure you don't. Nevertheless, these tools won't work unless you pick them up in the first place. Peace of mind is not hard to find, it's just about doing (and thinking about) things differently.

I can only hope that you get as much pleasure from your new tools as I do. Thank you for your time and I wish you well on your journey of happiness.

Dave Lee
The Hairy Arsed Builder

Can also be found on Facebook.
https://www.facebook.com/thehairyarsedbuilder

The Hairy Arsed Builder's Guide to Stress Management, authored by former builder Dave Lee, is a DIY guide with a difference. Working within the construction industry for 25 years, Dave was no stranger to the strain caused by his chosen occupation and wrote the guide with the intention of helping others combat the strains caused by everyday life.

Dave had a troubled start in life and he experienced a childhood in and out of care. He entered jail for the first time at the age of 15 and this became a regular occurrence throughout his teenage years up until the age of 21. After being sent to a bail hostel at the age of 21 he started to make positive steps towards a change in his thinking. Building a career and improving his life became a priority for Dave.

However, throughout his life Dave battled with an alcohol problem.

In 2006 Dave reached rock bottom. He was deeply unhappy and depressed, drinking heavily and was facing the break up of his marriage. In addition to this, as he progressed up the construction career ladder, he became no stranger to the strain caused by his chosen profession and often felt emotionally, physically and spiritually broken. It was then that he made a conscious decision to turn his life around and he spent the next five years of his life on a journey of self discovery.

Dave tried countless solutions for his problems over the years and worked his way through many books and courses in a bid to relieve himself of stress, bouts of depression and heavy drinking sessions. He noticed that many of the people with whom he worked suffered from the same problems and issues as he did, and he wanted to help them.

Dave did so for many years by talking to other builders on sites around Britain and sharing the tools that he discovered so that they too could benefit.

Wanting to reach a wider audience, Dave decided he needed to start writing. So Dave Lee became the Hairy Arsed Builder and The Hairy Arsed Builder's Guide to Stress Management was born.

As Dave began to publicise the guide, he found that it was not just builders who appreciated his work. School children found it was something they could read, understand and apply to their lives, as did housewives, and people from all walks of life.

Dave uses builder's terminology throughout The Hairy Arsed Builder's Guide to Stress Management which makes the concepts within it easier to grasp. It is divided into chapters which resonate with the reader and form the building blocks of the guide. The chapters include Planning, Foundations, Drainage, Hard Graft, Driving, Bills, Bills and more Bills, Work in Progress, Tea Break and Decorating. Each provides an essential tool and comes with a story that illustrates the concept graphically. The guide has been very well received from people in the building trade and also within the consumer market.

In addition to his guide, Dave has now started a project called The Infinity Foundation. The project aims to work with teenagers to improve their self esteem and personal responsibility with the vision of improving their outlook on life. Dave has also won the 2013 Guardian Constructive Carers Award after being nominated by the Kids Company, for services to charitable causes and advancing philanthropic endeavours of others.